T0197113

LET'S GET STARTED

Bible Lessons for Discussion

Dawaw

LET'S GET STARTED
BIBLE LESSONS FOR DISCUSSION

iUniverse books may be ordered through booksellers or by contacting:

iUniverse
1663 Liberty Drive
Bloomington, IN 47403
www.iuniverse.com
1-800-Authors (1-800-288-4677)

ISBN: 978-1-5320-2909-7 (sc)
ISBN: 978-1-5320-2910-3 (e)

Library of Congress Control Number: 2017916079

Print information available on the last page.

iUniverse rev. date: 10/25/2017

This exercise booklet guides the study of embracing Christian living on earth and attaining eternal life. After completing these self-paced exercises, you will have a better understanding of the Christian lifestyle/Christian walk.

This exercise booklet may generate many questions. Like many other publications, all the answers are not found in this booklet. A reprint of the entire BIBLE would be needed to do that. You are encouraged to make a list of questions as you study. Search the scriptures and discuss issues with others; such as your study group, pastor, family, and friends.

It cannot be stressed enough how important it is for you to get into or continue BIBLE study. Do not confuse the study of the BIBLE with how you approached academic studies. Life is less predictable and requires spiritual guidance. The study tools may be similar, but be prepared to study for your 'life-time'. Do not strive for knowledge only—get understanding; i.e., learn to apply and to use that knowledge appropriately. There will be no graduation from the study of the BIBLE. You will be a student forever. Your gift for dedication to your studies will be a firm belief that is supported by scriptures and some wisdom to enhance living the Christian lifestyle.

OBJECTIVES

- To provide an introduction into the study of the Bible
- To provide some study tools
- To stimulate and motivate continued study of the Bible
- To review commonly used scriptures and associated terms/phrases

The main objective for this booklet is to build or improve the Christian foundation and to encourage keeping faith while persevering/pushing forward. In general, it will

1. Examine personal roles as Christians and as members of the church and the community.
2. Determine what GOD will have us to do.
3. Identify principles (commands and promises) from GOD that will lead to a more spiritual life on earth and to an eternal life.
4. Provide sound doctrine that will:
   a. Enable us to make an informed decision to live a Christian life;
   b. Encourage us to learn and to exemplify Christian principles, whereby strengthening our faith while striving for eternal life;
   c. Stimulate us to love unconditionally as we share the WORD
   d. Lead us to encourage each other spiritually as we endure this race on earth; and
   e. Serve as a source of quick and easy references.

CONTENTS

Each Lesson Includes:

1. A <u>brief description</u> of the topic along with its purpose and functions.
2. Key <u>Scripture passages</u> that support the topic, and serve as a helpful resource for future reference.
3. <u>Research questions</u> designed to gain a better understanding of the topic and its application in everyday living.
4. <u>Something to review</u> to help begin processing the new knowledge and learning to apply it into relationships with others.
5. Space for <u>journaling</u> comments and/or questions.

The <u>Bonus Section</u> gives a snapshot that helps to simplify the understanding of the Book of Revelation.

STUDY TOOLS

A. Prepare before study time:
   1. Items needed (see item B1. below)
   2. Time (uninterrupted and specific)
   3. Quiet place
   4. Clear and open-mind (free from daily worries and activities)

B. During study time, pray and:
   1. Have on hand:
      a. Bible (preferably with a concordance, references, dictionary)
      b. Biblical dictionary
      c. Commentary
      d. Pencil and paper
      e. Of course, online search engines [goggle, bing, etc.] are quite useful
   2. Read the entire chapter for best insight (not just 1 or 2 verses of scriptures).
   3. Look up any unfamiliar words.
   4. Refer to a commentary for clarification.
   5. Make notes for future references.
   6. List questions for your teacher/study group.

When you study with a group, these are important:
1. Attendance
2. Attention
3. Participation, and
4. Cooperation.
   Be present and on time; actively listen, comment, and ask questions; and be decent and in order.

C. After study time, pray and ask GOD for understanding and wisdom, then meditate on what you studied.

LESSON ONE

THE BIBLE

The Bible gives to us the gospel (good news) from GOD. Hebrews 8:10-12 states that his gospel puts divine laws in our minds and writes them in our hearts; it tells us we will be HIS people and HE our GOD; that we will know HIM; HE will be merciful unto us; and HE will forgive our sins and lawlessness.

The Bible reveals GOD's plan for us. It provides HIS instructions for us to gain salvation and HIS promise of eternal life. It also provides HIS promise of eternal damnation for sinners (those who reject HIM). It was given to fill our minds and hearts, which would then guide our choices/decisions. The Bible provides methods and procedures to transform and to maintain a Christian lifestyle. It helps to produce faith, to encourage us, and to make us wise.

The Bible contains 66 books that were divinely inspired and authored by more than 40 writers. According to II Timothy 3:16 scriptures are given by inspiration of GOD. And, the Holy Spirit is the divine producer of the scripture (II Peter 1:20-21). These books contain history, biography, poetry, letters, laws, parables, hymns, prophecy, drama, etc. that is known as scripture. For example: in the 27 books of the New Testament, the first four books (The Gospels) contain the life of Jesus; the book of Acts of the Apostles details how to be saved and receive the Holy Spirit; the next 21 books describes how to live a Christian life; and the last book (Revelation) tells of the return of Jesus and eternal life in GOD's Kingdom.

Purpose of scripture:

1. Salvation to Believers (Romans 1:16-17)
2. Quick, Powerful, and a Discerner (Hebrews 4:12)
3. It Endureth Forever (I Peter 1:24-25
4. Hear and Receive (John 12:47-48)
5. Its Inspiration and Its Power (II Timothy 3:15-17)

Find the Truth in Scriptures: Write your personal definition of the Bible and include scripture to support your thoughts.

For example: The Bible is our instructions for developing and maintaining proper relationships while on earth. According to Exodus 20 (The Ten Commandments), the first four commandments explain our relationship with GOD; the remaining six explain our relationships with each other and the things GOD created. Also, John 13:34 gives us the commandment from Jesus to love one another.

_____
_____
_____
_____
_____
_____
_____
_____
_____
_____
_____
_____
_____
_____
_____
_____

Something to Review

Subject: "Symbols used to describe Scriptures"

1. Hammer to convict (Jeremiah 23:29)
2. Fire to refine (Jeremiah 23:29)
3. Mirror to reflect (James 1:23)
4. Seed to multiply (I Peter 1:23)
5. Laver to cleanse (Ephesians 5:26)
6. Lamp to guide (Psalm 119:105)
7. Rain and snow to refresh (Isaiah 55:10)
8. Sword to cut (Hebrews 4:12; Ephesians 6:17)
9. Bow for revenge (Habaka 3:9)
10. Gold to enrich (Psalm 19:7-10)
11. Power to create faith and eternal life (Romans 10:17; I Peter 1:23)
12. Food to nourish
    Milk for babes—I Peter 2:2;
    Bread for the hungry—Matthew 4:4;
    Meat For men—Hebrew 5:11-14;
    Honey for dessert—Psalm 19:10

Excerpt from Holy Bible KJV,
Thomas Nelson Inc
12 *Symbols of the Word of GOD*
Page 433-1

THE TRINITY

The concept of one GOD who is three spirits is widely recognized among Christians. Each (GOD, the Father; The Word; and the Holy Spirit) has the ability to function independently of the other. I John 5:7 states," *For there are three that bear record in heaven: the Father, the Word, and the Holy Ghost; and these three are one*". This idea is further supported by John 1:1-3, "*In the beginning was the Word, and the Word was with God, and the Word was God. The same was in the beginning with GOD. All things were made by him; and without him was not anything made that was made.*"

However, some Christians believe these three are not one God but are totally separate and distinct spirits; GOD being the Almighty and Most High, who created the Word (Christ Jesus his only begotten son) and Jesus had a hand in creating the Holy Spirit. Here are some of the Scriptures that support this concept. John 3:16, "*For God so loved the world, that he gave his only begotten son, that whosoever believeth in him should not perish, but have everlasting life.*" Colossians 1:15-17, "*Who is the image of the invisible GOD, the firstborn of every creature: For by him were all things created, that are in heaven, and that are in earth, visible and invisible, whether they be throne or dominions, or principalities, or powers: all things were created by him and for him: And he is before all things, and by him all things consist.*" John 14:28, "*Ye have heard how I said unto you, I go away, and come again unto you. If ye loved me, ye would rejoice, because I said, I go unto the Father: for my Father is greater than I.*"

Consider the thought that as humans, we sometimes apply carnal/ logical thinking to spiritual situations; forgetting that GOD is Almighty and is able to accomplish what humans cannot conceive. Isaiah 55:8, 9, 11 states, *"For my thoughts are not your thoughts, neither are your ways my ways, saith the Lord. For as the heavens are higher than the earth, so are my ways higher than your ways, and my thoughts than your thoughts...So shall my word be that goeth forth out of my mouth: it shall not return unto me void, but it shall accomplish that which I please, and it shall prosper in the thing whereto I sent it."*

GOD/In Hebrew language is YHWH [creator of everything; our Supreme Being; The Almighty and Most High]

1. HIS name is Jehovah (Exodus 6:3; Psalms 83:18; Isaiah 12:2, 26:4)
2. Guides by righteousness and compassion (Psalms 23)
3. Only one GOD (I Corinthians 8:5,6)
4. GOD's delight (Jeremiah 9:23)
5. What believer are to GOD (I Peter 2:5, 9,10)
6. To please GOD (Hebrews 13)
7. Trust HIM (Psalms 125:1)
8. Things GOD hates (Proverbs 6:16-19)
9. HIS will for man (Matthew 18:14; I Timothy 2:4; II Peter 3:9; John 3:16)

The Word/Christ Jesus [creator of all things heavenly and earthly; redeemer of the soul of man; only begotten Son of GOD]

1. Came from Heaven to earth (John 1:1-5)
2. Purpose of His work (Titus 2:14)
3. To judge all (John 5:22)
4. What Christ is to believers (I Peter 2:3, 4, 6)
5. What Christ is to sinners (I Peter 2:7, 8)

Holy Spirit/Holy Ghost [producer of Scripture; executor of the Divine Will of GOD as it relates to man]

1. Purpose (Romans 8:6, 14-16, 26-27; 2 Corinthians 3:6)
2. Work of the Holy Spirit (John 16:7-15; 2 Timothy 3:15)
3. Given to believers (Romans 5:5; Acts 15:8)
4. Renews (Titus 3:4-7)

Find the Truth in Scriptures: What is GOD's, The Almighty and Most High, name? What are some of HIS titles? Note scriptures you find to support your answer.

_____
_____
_____
_____
_____
_____
_____
_____
_____
_____
_____
_____
_____
_____
_____
_____
_____
_____
_____
_____
_____

Something to Review

Subject: "Do You Know Jesus?"

John 7:25-28

Then said some of them of Jerusalem, Is not this he, whom they seek to kill? But, lo, he speaketh boldly, and they say nothing unto him. Do the rulers know indeed that this is the very Christ? Howbeit we know this man whence he is: but when Christ cometh, no man knoweth whence he is.

How to tell when man does not know Jesus:
- He is an instigator. He is a trouble maker that starts confusion.
- He wants to be a part of the in-crowd. He takes the most popular view point at that time.
- He does not understand Jesus' ways of doing things. He thinks with a carnal mind and not with a spiritual mind.
- He only repeats what he has heard, never what he knows.
- He has a false perception of who Jesus really is because he has not taken the time to really get to know Him.

When man knows Jesus:
- He is filled with the Holy Spirit (Romans 8:5-10)
- He cannot serve two masters [man, devil, or GOD] at the same time (Matthew 6:24)
- He has a love for everyone (I John 4:7-8)
- He hunger and thirst after righteousness (Matthew 5:6)
- He knows that the tongue is powerful (James 3:5-14)

LESSON THREE

COVENANT

In the Bible, a covenant is an agreement based upon commitments and is used for the relationship between man and GOD. It typically involves promises and obligations from both man and GOD. For example, one covenant with Abram [Abraham] can be found in Genesis 12:1-3. *"Now the LORD had said unto Abram, Get thee out of thy country, and from thy kindred, and from thy father's house, unto a land that I will shew thee: And I will make of thee a great nation, and I will bless thee, and make thy name great; and thou shalt be a blessing; And I will bless them that bless thee, and curse him that curseth thee; and in thee shall all families of the earth be blessed."*

In addition, a covenant identifies why the agreement/relationship is being formed. Another factor of a covenant addresses the general conditions that will govern the agreement and how man is to act or react. Rewards for maintaining the agreement and penalties in the event of the failure of man to up hold his end of the agreement are defined. Keep in mind that GOD assures us that HIS word will not return void. So, we do not have to worry about or doubt HIS commitments and promises to us.

Some Churches have covenants as well as vision and mission statements. It is wise to read these documents to see how they relate to the Word of GOD before joining any congregation. When we join a congregation, by agreeing with these documents, we form a covenant with that congregation. Covenants, mission and vision statements should be sound Christian doctrines that incorporate the will of GOD in accordance with the teachings of Jesus and scripture.

Find the Truth in Scriptures: Review your church's vision and mission statements. Note scripture you find to support them? What evidence is there to show your congregation continually practices these covenants?

_____

_____

_____

_____

_____

_____

_____

_____

_____

_____

_____

_____

_____

_____

_____

_____

_____

_____

_____

_____

_____

_____

_____

_____

_____

Something to Review

Christ's {the new} covenant is better than Moses' {the old} covenant according to Hebrews 8:7-10:28.

OLD COVENANT		NEW COVENANT	
Through Moses	John 1:17	Through Christ	Hebrews 8:6; 9-15
By angels	Galatians 3:19	By the Holy Ghost	Hebrews 10:15-18
Annual atonement	Hebrews 10:3	Eternal atonement	Hebrews 10:14
By works	Romans 4:13	By Grace	John 1:17
Christ ended	Romans 10:4	Christ Started	Hebrews 8:6; 10:9
Could not redeem	Hebrews 10:4	Redeems	Galatians 3:13; Heb 9:12-15
Gave death	2 Corinthians 3:7	Gave life	Romans 8:2; Gal 3
Live according to works	Galatians 3:10	Live according to Faith	Galatians 3:11
Makes guilty	2 Corinthians 3:9	Makes free	Galatians 5:1; John 8
Natural	Hebrews 9:10-13	Spiritual	II Corinthians 3:6,13
No eternal life	Romans 4:13	Eternal life	Hebrews 9:15
No mercy	Hebrews 10:28	Complete mercy	Hebrews 8:12
No personal access to GOD	Hebrews 9:7	Personal access to GOD	Hebrews 4:14-16; 10-17
No salvation	Hebrews 10:2-4	Eternal Salvation	Hebrews 4:9; 10-10
Remembers sin	Hebrews 10:3	Sin forgiven	Hebrews 8:12; 10:17
Was fulfilled	Matthews 5:17-18	Now in force	Hebrews 8:6; 10:9

Excerpt from Holy Bible KJV,
Thomas Nelson Inc
85 Old and New Covenant Contrasts
Page 351-NT

LESSON FOUR

FAITH

Faith is a state of mind in which a person places his trust and reliance on something or someone. Christian faith is not based on logic or material evidence. Christian faith is not simply being obedient. It is the understanding of and living life based on Scriptures and the teachings of Jesus Christ. It is the acceptance of GOD's will and His promises. It is knowing that the alliance between man and Jesus provides freedom from condemnation. And, it is through everyday experiences that this faith is made strong and unshakeable. Even when things seem to be only going wrong in our lives or when nothing seems right, Faith should be exercised to get through these times. Faith (a sense of complete trust and belief in Christ) is necessary to our salvation (Mark16:16). GOD's grace and mercy is granted through our faith in the death and resurrection of Jesus Christ.

Faith is the gift of GOD. Its components include:
- Spiritual – an internal force sustained by the Spirit of GOD
- Intellectual – recognizing the truth of GOD
- Emotional – asserting to the truth
- Volitional – trusting in that truth

1. Defined (Hebrews 11:1)
2. Is Necessary (Hebrew 11:6)
3. Faith without works (James 2:14-19)
4. Faith by hearing (Romans 10:17)

5. Justified by faith (Romans 3:27-28)
6. Shield of faith (Ephesians 6:16)
7. Work of faith (I Thessalonians 1:3; II Thessalonians 1:11)
8. Without faith (Hebrews 11:6)

Find the Truth in Scriptures: A preacher's wife became extremely ill and required long term care. The cost of her medical care each month exceeded their monthly income. They received some support from family, friends, churches, etc. However, that generosity soon ended. In order to care for her, the preacher sold their possessions and began to use his tithes to help meet her needs. Two years later the situation was still the same, so he continued to not pay tithes. Some Christians have been taught to pay tithes first from their earnings/income, be patient, and have faith that the LORD will provide their needs. Do you feel the preacher lost faith in GOD providing? Should he have paid his tithes? What would you have done? What answers can you find in the Scriptures?

_____

_____

_____

_____

_____

_____

_____

_____

_____

_____

_____

_____

_____

_____

_____

_____

_____

Something to Review

Subject: "Responding to Problems"

Job: 1:6-12

Now there was a day when the sons of GOD came to present themselves before the LORD, and satan came also among them. And the LORD said unto satan, Whence comest thou? Then Satan answered the LORD, and said, From going to and fro in the earth, and from walking up and down in it. And the LORD said unto Satan, Hast thou considered my servant Job, That there is none like him in the earth, A perfect and an upright man, one that feareth GOD, and escheweth evil? Then satan answered the LORD, and said, Doth Job fear God for naught? Hast not thou made an hedge about him, and about his house, And about all that he hath on every side? Thou hast blessed the work of his hands, and his substance is increased in the land. But put forth thine hand now, and touch all that he hath, and he will curse thee to thy face. And the LORD said unto Satan, Behold, all that he hath is in thy power; only upon himself put not forth thine hand. So Satan went forth from the presence of the LORD.

Sometimes man responds to the symptoms of a problem rather than the problem itself. A problem occurs when the situation we are in is not the situation we want to be in. Man is more apt to lose faith and/or give up when he respond to symptoms of life challenges rather than addressing the real problem. Satan's problem is that he wants to be supreme/a GOD. The things that he did and does to man are symptoms of that problem.

Satan

- Wanted to be in charge—above all others
- Did not want to nor offered to help GOD but wanted to take over
- Vain; all about himself
- Jealous and envious of GOD and HIS faithful servants
- Strives to put others down. However, he has to think they are better than he is, in order to want to bring them down.
- A deceiver—he wanted Job to think that GOD had deserted and caused him harm so that Job would curse GOD.

(continues on next page)

Subject: "Responding to Problems"
(continued)

GOD
- Is all knowing
    - o He knew the strengths and commitment of Job
    - o He knew Satan's problem and how to handle him
- Suggested Job and set the boundaries for the trial
    - o He had confidence in Job because of the way he lived
    - o He gave Satan free reign to do anything to test Job except kill him
- Allowed the trial of Job
    - o To conform Job's life more to HIS plan
    - o To allow Satan an opportunity to be faithful
    - o To put Satan in his place
    - o To encourage others to trust HIM
    - o To show the difference our faith can make when life seems unfair

LESSON FIVE

PRAYER

All of us at some point have needed to go to our parent(s) to request help, forgiveness, or to thank them. The same is the desire of Christians to go to GOD (The Father, Jehovah, The Almighty and Most High). This communication with GOD is called a prayer. However, prayer to The Father is always done in the name of HIS Son, Jesus Christ; as it is only through Him that Christians have access to GOD at all.

A prayer is not a learned speech or recital. It is spiritual. During this communication, man can open his heart and mind to make a devout petition to GOD or he can receive an answer to his requests. A prayer can be personal, on behalf of another, or for the soul of a dead person. Prayers can include confessions, thanksgiving, praise and adoration, requests for blessings, or requests for divine intervention. Prayer is important because it glorifies and builds a closeness with GOD. And, for man, it is a privilege. There is no set number of prayers required of man. He is free to talk with GOD anytime, anywhere, and as often as he feels the need or want. There are no boundaries on what man can or cannot request or tell GOD.

1. Pray every where (I Timothy 2:8)
2. How to pray (Luke 11:1-13; Matthews 6:5-15)
3. Pray and believe (Mark 11:24)
4. Pray always (Luke 18:1)
5. Ask in Jesus name (John 14:12-15; John 16:23-26)

15

6. Prayer and fasting (Mark 9:28-29; Matthew 6:16-18)
7. Pray continually (Acts 6:4)
8. Prayer of faith (James 5:15)
9. Prayer of a righteous man (James 5:16)
10. Prayers of saints (Revelations 5:8)
11. Pray for all (I Timothy 2:1-4)

Find the Truth in Scriptures :

In the Bible, how often and under what circumstances did Jesus pray?
Note scripture you find to support your answer.

_____
_____
_____
_____
_____
_____
_____
_____
_____
_____
_____
_____
_____
_____
_____
_____
_____
_____
_____

Something to Review

"The Model Prayer"

Matthews 6:1-8

*Take heed that ye do not your alms
before men,
to be seen of them: Otherwise ye have no
reward of your Father which is in heaven.
Therefore when thou doest thine alms,
do not sound a trumpet before thee,
As the hypocrites do in the synagogues
and in the streets,
That they may have glory of men. Verily I
say unto you, They have their reward.
But when thou doest alms, let not thy left
hand know what thy right hand doeth:
That thine alms may be in secret: and thy
Father which seeth in secret himself
Shall reward thee openly. And when thou
prayest, thou shalt not be as The hypocrites
are; for they love to pray standing in the
synagogues
And in the corners of the streets,
that they may be seen of men.
Verily I say unto you, They have their reward.
But thou, when thou prayest, enter into
thy closet, and when thou hast shut Thy
door, pray to thy Father which is in secret;
and Thy Father which seeth in secret shall
reward thee openly.
But when ye pray, use not vain repetitions.
As the heathen do; For they think that they
shall be heard for their much speaking.
Be not ye therefore like unto them;
for your Father knoweth what things ye
have need of, before ye ask him*

Pray a Fervent Prayer
- Wholehearted, with humility and honesty
- Close your mind and heart to the world and concentrate on GOD
- Not for popularity or recognition from man
- Not rehearsed nor a performance

(continues on next page)

"The Model Prayer"
(continued)

Matthews 6:9-13

After this manner therefore pray ye:
Our Father which art in heaven,
Hollowed be thy name.
Thy kingdom come.
Thy will be done in earth,
as it is in heaven.
Give us this day our daily bread.
And forgive us our debts,
as we forgive our debtors.
And lead us not into temptation,
but deliver us from evil:
For thine is the kingdom,
and the power,
and the glory, for ever.
A-men.

During prayer:
- Humble yourself and clear your mind of obstructions before going to GOD
- Acknowledge GOD: HIS holiness and reign should put you into focus and keep your mind on who you are talking with
- Let GOD know that you are in agreement with HIS promise of eternal life. This increases your sense of hope. It encourages obedience to carry out the will of GOD in your life.
- Live and enjoy the day because it was made and given by the LORD. Tomorrow is not promised.
- Ask for immediate needs not just wants.
- Ask everything from GOD because you seek GOD's guidance in everything and not because of a need or want
- Ask for forgiveness and to forgive others. There is nothing like a clear conscience.
- Ask for divine protection from everyday life; prepare/equip your mind and heart to be guided by the Holy Spirit all day
- Praise and glorify GOD
- Always ask GOD to hear your prayer "in Jesus' name".

SALVATION AND BAPTISM

In these last days, times are hard. As humans, we are faced with situations throughout our life time that cause problems, some dangerous even life threatening. In fact, some people could face temptations on a daily basis. Job 14:1 states. *"Man that is born of a woman is of few days, and full of trouble."* But, isn't it great to know that when Jesus Christ died for our sins, He provided a way that man would not suffer eternally. Salvation is the saving of man's soul from an eternity in hell to an everlasting life with GOD Almighty. And, salvation is granted by GOD through HIS grace and believers faith in Jesus (His death, burial and resurrection as GOD's only begotten son). Salvation is not based on the merits of man's good deeds/works, birth rights, creed, or nationality, etc. Man cannot purchase, borrow, or transfer salvation. However, good deeds/works are evidence of man's conformity to the will of GOD and man's faith in the promise of salvation.

After accepting Christ as Lord and Savior, baptism is another way man shows his faith in the promise of salvation. Baptism is an appeal [by man] to GOD to take away the guilt of past sins. This outward showing represents an inward cleansing. And, through this cleansing, man becomes a new person. His old nature dies and he walks in a newness of life in Christ. Following baptism, man identifies himself as a part of the body of Christ [The Church] and shows his continued gratefulness/gratitude by living a Christian life.

1. GOD's will (I Timothy 2:1-4; 2 Peter 3:9; John 3:16)
2. Must be born again (I Peter 1:19-23 John 3:1-7)
3. Baptized into one body (I Corinthians 12:13-14)
4. Redemption for sin (Acts 2:19-21; Roman 10:10; Colossians 2:11-13)
5. Grow in grace and knowledge of Jesus (2 Peter 3:18)
6. Method of deliverance from sin (Romans 6:1-14; Ephesians 2:8-10)
7. Water baptism (Mark 1:4; Luke 3:3)
8. Spirit baptism (Mark 1:7,8; Luke 3:16; John 1:32-34; 7:37-39)

Find the Truth in Scriptures: Is there a difference between being saved from sins through baptism; being saved when we become Christians; and being saved when Jesus returns? When do we actually become saved? Note scripture you find to support your answer.

_____

_____

_____

_____

_____

_____

_____

_____

_____

_____

_____

_____

_____

_____

_____

Something to Review

"Why be baptized?"

<u>Acts 2:38</u> *Then Peter said unto them, Repent, and be baptized every one of you in the name of Jesus Christ for the remission of sins, and ye shall receive the gift of the Holy Spirit.*

<u>Romans 6:1-6</u> *What shall we say then? Shall we continue in sin, that grace may abound? God forbid. How shall we, that are dead to sin, live any longer therein? Know ye not, that so many of us as were baptized into Jesus Christ were baptized into his death? Therefore we are buried with him by baptism into death: that like as Christ was raised up from the dead by the glory of the Father, even so we also should walk in newness of life. For if we have been planted together in the likeness of his death, we shall be also in the likeness of his resurrection: Knowing this, that our old man is crucified with him, that the body of sin might be destroyed, that henceforth we should not serve sin.*

<u>Galatians 3:27</u> *For as many of you as have been baptized into Christ, have put on Christ.*

<u>1 Peter 3:21</u> *The like figure whereunto even baptism doth also now save us (not the putting away of the filth of the flesh, but the answer of a good conscience toward God.) by the resurrection of Jesus Christ.*

LESSON SEVEN

CHRISTIANS

Those who believe that Christ Jesus is Lord are considered Christians. In addition,

- they follow His example of lifestyle, teachings, and doctrines
- they embrace righteousness
- they are servants of and are acceptable with GOD
- they have a hunger and thirst for GOD's Word (Scriptures)
- they yearn to have GOD reign in their lives
- they have a desire to be obedient to GOD's will
- they strive to edify GOD's people.

The Christian's responsibility is to get their heart and mind in tune with what GOD wants done. Romans 12:1-2 states, *"I beseech you therefore, brethren, by the mercies of God, that ye present your bodies a living sacrifice, holy, acceptable unto God, which is your reasonable service. And be not conformed to this world: but be ye transformed by the renewing of your mind, that ye may prove what is that good, and acceptable, and perfect will of GOD."*

1. Walk after the spirit (Romans 8:1-13; Galatians 5:24-26)
2. Christian responsibilities (Romans 14:13-21)
3. Be imitators of GOD (Ephesians 5:1-2)
4. How others will know (John 13:34-35; 2 Corinthians 5:17-19)
5. How to grow spiritually (I Peter 2:2-4)

6. Our offering to GOD (Romans 12:1-2)
7. Christian living (Hebrews 13:1-6)
8. Fruit of the Spirit (Galatians 5:22-23)
9. Christian Conduct (Romans 12:9-12)

Find the Truth in Scriptures:

Read Ephesians 6:10-20 and explain its importance to everyday Christian Living. Note other scriptures that support your answer.

_____
_____
_____
_____
_____
_____
_____
_____
_____
_____
_____
_____
_____
_____
_____
_____
_____
_____
_____
_____
_____
_____

Something to Review

"Being Born Again"

Romans 12:1-5

*I beseech you therefore,
brethren,
by the mercies of GOD,
that ye present your
Bodies a living sacrifice, holy,
acceptable unto God,
Which is your reasonable
service.
And be not conformed to this
world; but be ye transformed by
the renewing of your mind,
That ye may prove what is that
good, and acceptable,
and perfect will of God.
For I say, through the grace
given unto me, to every man
that is among you,
Not to think of himself more
highly than he ought to think;
But to think soberly,
according as God hath dealt to
every man the measure of faith.
For as we have many members
in one body; and
all members have not the same
office:
So we, being many,
are one body in Christ,
And every one members one of
another.*

Your reasonable service (the least you should do) without the expectation of something in return; that is, out of love and obedience to GOD

- It begins within you; dedicate yourself using only the power and willingness the Lord has given to you
- You have the power to do something but trust GOD to handle it.
- Don't just get in the church but get into GOD
- Make the decision to follow the will of GOD and the teachings of Jesus
- Make your daily activities to be those of a Christian practice

Transformed by ending the old ways and starting a new life in Christ

- Start with your mind—thinking, attitude, conduct; you have to change your attitude in order to change your lifestyle
- Attitude dictates behavior in the form of actions and words
- Don't be righteous in your own mind
- Don't be arrogant or put yourself above others; there is no big 'I' and little 'you'.
- Stay focused on being a Christian; be well balanced in your thinking
- Measure your worth according to your faith in GOD; you are not expected to be able do every thing but do what you can with your measure of faith given by GOD

We are one body; drawing from and belonging to Christ and acceptable unto GOD.

- No one person is greater than the sum of all the members of the body of Christ.
- We are diverse in our desires, talents, and skills but expected to combine these differences to work as one in our Christian duties.

LESSON EIGHT

TITHES

Traditionally, tithing represents the free-will giving of a tenth of one's earnings as an offering to God. However, more than just the giving of money, it demonstrates our acceptance of GOD as our LORD and our desire to be obedient to His will. It is also a way of saying thank you to GOD because we are grateful for those things he has provided in our lives. Tithing has nothing to do with the law but everything to do with a grateful heart and love for GOD.

Tithes are often used for supporting the work of God through church or other religious institutes; providing for the administration and missionary workers; and, supporting those who are disadvantaged.

According to Luke 21:1-4, a man's spirit of giving (conduct, attitude, motive, etc.) is more important than what he gives.

GIVE:

1. As GOD has prospered (I Corinthians 16:2)
2. Cheerfully and with purpose (2 Corinthians 9:7)
3. Freely (Matthew 10:8; 2 Corinthians 9:6)
4. A good measure (Luke 6:38)
5. Willingly (2 Corinthians 8:12)

GIVE:

1. Glory to GOD (Revelation 14:7)
2. Don't give carelessly (Matthews 7:6)
3. Thanks (Ephesians 5:20; Colossians 3:17; I Thessalonians 5:18)
4. To the needy (Roman 12;13)
5. Time to GOD (I Timothy 4:13)
6. To whoever asks (Matthew 5:42)
7. Yourself wholly (I Timothy 4:13-16)

Find the Truth in Scriptures: Some Christians believe that casino gambling is a sin. Is there a difference between casino gambling and investing in a 401K or stock markets? Should tithes be paid on these types of winnings/earnings? Note scripture you find to support your answer.

_____

_____

_____

_____

_____

_____

_____

_____

_____

_____

_____

_____

_____

_____

_____

Something to Review

Tithing

Old Testament	New Testament
• To supply GOD's house (Malachi 3:10)	• Also needs justice, mercy, and faith (Matthew 23:23)
• To honor GOD (Proverb 3:9-10)	• Condemned sacrilege (Romans 2:22)
• For Levites (Numbers 18:21-24)	• Teachers to be paid (Galatians 6:6)
• For priests (Numbers 18:26; Nehemiah 10:37; 12:44)	• Ordained minister support (I Corinthians 9:7-14; I Timothy 6:17-19)
• For poor and ministers every 3 years (Deuteronomy 14:27-29; 26:12-14)	• Give as GOD prospers (I Corinthians 16:2)
	• Proof of obedience and appreciation of GOD's blessings (Hebrews 7:5-10)

Excerpt from Holy Bible KJV,
Thomas Nelson Inc
The Doctrine of Tithing
Page 61 NT

CHURCH

The church provides a place for worship, praise, fellowship, and encouragement. It provides teaching and preaching of the Christian doctrines. It can teach things that man would never learn on his own. It is the vessel that helps Christians to develop a sense of belonging to a spiritually secure family through their involvement with other believers. The Church is the community of GOD's people, those who identify themselves as believers [the body of Christ, also called The Church]. They live according to GOD's will; HIS laws; and HIS forgiveness, acceptance, and love.

Although the church is commonly self governed, its leaders' main objective is to be servants of Christ and its function is to praise and glorify GOD. The time, resources, and abilities of dedicated believers are needed to fulfill the work and mission of the church. GOD has given different abilities to different believers, and HE wants all believers to work together for the common good of everyone. These dedicated believers are essential in order for the church to effectively reflect the works of Jesus and his love for the world.

1. Belongs to GOD/Christ (Matthew 16:17-18; Ephesians 2:19-22; 5:25-29)
2. Foundation (Ephesians 2:19-22; I Corinthians 3:11; 12:27,28)
3. Confirms the word (Mark 16:15-20; Romans 15:18-21, 29)
4. Maintain sound doctrine and Christian living (Romans 16:17-18; I Corinthians 7:17)

5. Maintain perfect unity (Roman 12:16; I Corinthians 1:10; Ephesians 4:1-6; I Peter 3:8)

6. Evangelizes (Matthew 28:19-20; Mark 16:15-20)

Sabbath Number Four of the Ten Commandments states to remember and keep the Sabbath Holy. According to The New Testament, Christians are free to keep any day as Sabbath.

- (Romans 14:5-6)*One man esteemeth one day above another: another esteemeth every day alike. Let every man be fully persuaded in his own mind. He that regardeth the day, regardeth it unto the Lord; and he that regardeth not the day, to the Lord he doth not regard it. He that eateth, eateth to the Lord, for he giveth God thanks; and he that eateth not, to the Lord he eateth not, and giveth God thanks.*

- (Colossians 2:14-17)*Blotting out the handwriting of ordinances that was against us, which was contrary to us, and took it out of the way, nailing it to his cross: And having spoiled principalities and powers, he made a shew of them openly, triumphing over them in it. Let no man therefore judge you in meat, or in drink, or in respect of an holyday, or of the new moon, or of the Sabbath days; Which are a show of things to come; but the body is of Christ.*

Find the Truth in Scriptures: What involvement or responsibility should the church have in the community? Note scripture you find to support your answer.

_____

_____

_____

_____

Something to Review

Subject: "Traditions"

Mark 7:1-9

*Then came together unto him
the Pharisees, and certain of the
scribes,which came from Jerusalem.
And when they saw some of his disciples
eat bread with defiled, that is to say,
With unwashen, hands, they found fault.
For the Pharisees, and all the Jews,
Except they wash their hands oft, eat
not, holding the tradition of the elders.
And when they came from the market,
except they wash, they eat not. And
many other
Things there be, which they have received
to hold, as the washing of cups, and pots,
Brazen vessels, and of tables. Then the
Pharisees and scribes asked him,
Why walk not thy
Disciples according to the tradition of the
elders, but eat bread with unwashen hands?
He answered and said unto them, Well
hath Esaias prophesied of you hypocrites, as
it is written, This people honoureth me with
their lips, but their heart is far from me.
Howbeit in vain do they worship
me, teaching for doctrines the
commandments of men.
For laying aside the commandment of
GOD, ye hold the tradition of me, as the
washing of pots
And cups: and many other such things
ye do. And he said unto them, Full well
ye reject
The commandment of GOD, that ye may
keep your own tradition.*

Traditions are beliefs or customs that have been taught through the generations. Some traditions appear on the surface to be in accordance with scripture. But, when we examine their origins and procedures, we find they may have been created to place restrictions or boundaries on the people; or, they may be simple practices/rituals that have been handed down for generations. For example, many people go to church every Sunday because they were taught it is proper to do so in our society. They do not attend church with the intention of worship, praise, or love for the LORD. It's simply what one should do on Sunday. One way to find out if the practice of a tradition is of the Bible is to measure it by Scripture. Is it of GOD?

In this scripture, the people
o Honored GOD outwardly but not with the heart; vain worship
o Disobeyed GOD's commandment
o Kept traditions because they were taught by the elders (its always been done this way)
o Created and taught their own doctrines as commandments (making it easier isn't always better)

How do these statements fit into traditions or Scripture?
• Communion is served only on the first Sunday of each month and only to those baptized
• Tithing is 10% of gross earnings from jobs only; it does not include gifts, inheritance, winnings, etc.
• The celebration of holidays such as, Mothers/Fathers day, Easter, Christmas
• Babies should not be baptized

BONUS
BOOK OF REVELATION
[AT A GLANCE]

Revelation [at a glance]
"Condition of the world" (vv. 2:1 – 3:22)

	The concern	The Charge	Jesus' Promise
Ephesius *The Loveless Church*	Labored, persevered, patient, and have not become weary; nevertheless, have left their first love	Remember from whence you have fallen; Repent and do the first works	To eat from the tree of life, which is in the midst of the Paradise of GOD (He holds the seven stars in His right hand)
Smyrna *The Persecuted Church*	Suffered tribulation, poverty, and fear of prison	Be faithful until death	The crown of life and will not be hurt by the second death (The First and the Last, who was dead, and come to life)
Pergamos *The Compromising Church*	Held fast to Jesus' name and did not deny His faith; but some hold the doctrine of idol gods	Repent and overcome; or be stricken with the sword of Jesus' mouth	To eat some of the hidden manna; a white stone with a new name which no one knows except him who receives it (He has the sharp two-edged sword)
Thyatira *The Corrupt Church*	Allows false teaching and seduction to commit sexual immorality and sacrifices to idols	Hold to the doctrine of Jesus; and He will not add other burden	Will give power over the nations and will give the morning star (He has eyes like a flame of fire, and His feet like fine brass)

Sardis *The Dead Church*	Have a name that you are alive, but are dead	Be watchful and strengthen the things which remain; remember how you have received and heard, hold fast and repent	Shall be clothed in white garments, name will not be blotted out from the Book of Life, and He will confess the name before GOD and the angles (He has the seven Spirits of GOD and the seven stars)
Philadelphia *The faithful Church*	Kept Jesus' word and have not denied His name; Kept His command to persevere	Hold fast what you have	Will make them a pillar in the temple of GOD and go out no more; will write on him the name of GOD, the new city and His new name (He who is holy, He who is true)
Laodicea *The lukewarm Church*	Neither cold nor hot, lukewarm because they are rich and have no need of nothing	Buy gold refined in the fire from Jesus, to become rich, clothed in white garments, and anoint your eyes with eye salve, that you may see; be zealous and repent	Will grant to sit with Him on His throne (the Amen, the Faithful and True Witness, the Beginning of the creation of GOD)

Revelation [at a glance]
"Worship In Heaven" (vv. 4:1 – 5:14)

The Throne Room of Heaven

- A throne and One sat on it (His appearance like a jasper and a sardius stone)
- A rainbow around the throne (appearance like an emerald)
- Twenty-four Elders on thrones around the One (clothed in white robes; gold crowns on their heads)
- Seven burning lamps before the throne (which are the Seven spirits of GOD)
- A sea of glass, like crystal, before the throne
- Four Living Creatures in the midst of the throne and around (full of eyes in front and back; each had six wings)
  - First creature like a lion
  - Second creature like a calf
  - Third creature had a face like a man
  - Fourth creature like a flying eagle

The Lamb Takes the Scroll

- The Scroll
  - sealed with Seven Seals;
  - written inside and on the back;
  - no one under or on earth nor in heaven worthy to open or look at it
- The Lamb
  - stood in midst of the throne, the four living creatures, and the 24 elders as though it had been slain
  - had seven horns and seven eyes, which are Seven Spirits of GOD
  - the Lamb came and took the scroll in his right hand
- The four living creatures and the 24 elders fell down before the Lamb; each having a harp and golden bowls full of

incense (which are the prayers of the saints) and they sang a new song

- Voices of many angels, the living creatures, 24 elders, and thousands and thousands saying, *"Worthy is the Lamb who was slain to receive power and riches and wisdom, and strength and honor and glory and blessing!"*
- Every creature in heaven and on earth and under earth and in the sea, and all that are in them, said, *"Blessing and honor and glory and power be to Him who sits on the throne, and to the Lamb, forever and ever!"*
- Four living creatures said *"Amen!"*
- The twenty-four elders fell down and worshiped Him who lives forever and ever.

Revelation [at a glance]
"The Great Tribulation" (vv. 6:1-18:24)
The Lamb opens the Seven Seals

First Seal The Conqueror	• A white horse • He who sat on it had a bow and a crown was given to him • He went out conquering and to conquer
Second Seal Conflict on Earth	• A fiery red horse • It was granted to the one who sat on it to take peace from the earth and that people would kill one another and there was give to him a great sword
Third Seal Scarcity on Earth	• A black horse • He who sat on it had a pair of scales in his hand • From the midst of the four living creatures a voice says, "A quart of wheat for a demarius and 3 quarts of barley for a demarius and do not harm the oil and the wine
Fourth Seal Widespread Death on Earth	• A pale horse • He who sat on it was Death and Hades followed with him • Power was given them over a fourth of the earth to kill with a sword, with hunger, with death, and by the beasts of the earth
Fifth Seal The Cry of the Martyrs	• Under the altar, souls of those slain for the word of GOD and the testimony which they held • Each given a white robe and told to rest until both, the number of their fellow servants and their brethren would be killed as they were
Sixth Seal 1. Cosmic Disturbances	There was a great earthquake: • The sun became black as sackcloth of hair • The moon became like blood • Stars of heaven fell to the earth • The sky receded as a scroll when rolled up • Every mountain and island moved from its place • Every man hid in caves in the mountain rocks

Sixth Seal (continued) 2. The Sealed of Israel	• Four angels standing at the four corners of the earth holding the four winds of the earth granted to harm the earth and sea • One angel, ascending from the east, having the seal of GOD to seal 144,000 (12,000 from each of the twelve tribes) of all the tribes of the children of Israel on their foreheads before the four angels could harm the earth and sea
3. The Multitude from the Great Tribulation	• A multitude, which no one could number, of all nations, tribes, peoples, and tongues • Standing before the throne and the Lamb • Clothed with white robes, with palm branches in their hands (saying "Salvation belongs to our GOD….and to the Lamb") • They will serve GOD day and night in His temple • They shall not hunger nor thirst anymore; the sun shall not strike them nor any heat; the Lamb will shepherd them and lead them to living fountains of water; GOD shall wipe away every tear from their eyes
Seventh Seal Prelude to the Seven Trumpets	• Seven angels were given seven trumpets; they stood before GOD • Another angel having a golden censer, stood at the altar, was given much incense to offer with prayers before the throne. He filled the censer with fire from the altar and threw it to the earth. And, there were noises, thundering, lightnings, and an earthquake. • Then the seven angels prepared themselves to sound 1. Vegetation Struck Hail and fire mingled with blood were thrown to earth; a third of trees burned up and all green grass burned up 2. The Seas Struck Something like a great mountain burning with fire was thrown in the sea and a third of the sea became blood; a third of living creatures in the sea died; a third of ships were destroyed

Seventh Seal (continued) Prelude to the Seven Trumpets	3. The Waters Struck A great star (named wormwood) fell from heaven on a third of the rivers and the springs of water; a third of the waters became wormwood and many men died from the water 4. The Heavens Struck A third of the sun, a third of the moon, and a third of the stars were struck so a third of them were darkened; a third of the day did not shine likewise that night 5. The Locusts from the Bottomless Pit • A star fell from heaven to earth • He who was given the key to the bottomless pit, opened it: smoke arose and the sun and air were darkened; locust came out the smoke upon the earth and was given power as the scorpions and were commanded to only harm men who do not have the seal of GOD on their foreheads (not to kill but to torment for five months) 6. The Angels from the Euphrates The four angels bound at the great river of Euphrates were released to kill a third of mankind by the fire, the smoke, and brimstone of their mouths The Mighty Angel with the Little Rock Another angel from heaven clothed with a cloud, a rainbow on his head, a face like the sun, feet like pillars of fire, a little book open in his hand, sat his right foot on the sea and left on the land, cried out and seven thunders uttered their voices. The angel raised his hand to heaven and swore by GOD the time is near to reveal the mystery of GOD as He promised. The Two Witnesses They were to prophesy 1,260 days; clothed in sackcloth, with power over rain and water, power to devour their enemies, and power to release plagues on earth until they finish their testimony. The beast from the bottomless pit will kill them and their bodies lie in the streets of the great city where Jesus was crucified for three and a half days.

Men will rejoice and exchange gifts to celebrate their deaths. Then, breath of life from GOD will resurrect them; they ascend to heaven in a cloud. At the same hour there was a great earthquake and one-tenth of the city fell (7,000 people killed and the rest, afraid, gave glory to GOD).

7. The Kingdom Proclaimed
The kingdoms of this world become the kingdoms of our LORD and of His Christ, and He shall reign forever and ever.

The temple of GOD opened in heaven and the ark of His covenant was seen. There were lightnings, noises, thundering, an earthquake, and a great hail.

Revelation [at a glance]
"The Great Tribulation" (vv. 6:1-18:24)

Prelude to the Bowl Judgments

Seven angels having the seven last plagues, for in them the wrath of GOD is complete:

- Clothed in pure bright linen
- Their chests girded with golden bands
- One of the Four Living Creatures gave each a golden bowl full of the wrath of GOD to pour out on the earth

The Bowl Judgments

First Bowl: Loathsome Sores

- A foul and loathsome sore came upon the men who had the mark of the beast and those who worshipped his image

Second Bowl: The Sea Turns to Blood

- Sea became blood as a dead man and every living creature in the sea died

Third Bowl: The waters Turns to Blood

- Poured on the rivers and springs, and they became blood

Fourth Bowl: Men are Scorched

- Poured on the sun
- Power was given to him to scorch men with fire; and they blasphemed the name of GOD and did not repent and give Him glory

Fifth Bowl: Darkness and Pain

- Poured on the throne of the beast; his kingdom became dark; and they gnawed their tongues because of the pain and did not repent

Sixth Bowl: Euphrates Dried Up

- Poured on river Euphrates and it was dried up.
- Three unclean spirits came out the mouth of the dragon, the beast, and the false prophet to gather them to the battle of the great day of GOD Almighty at Armageddon

Seventh Bowl: The Earth Utterly Shaken

- Poured out into the air
- Caused thundering and lightnings, a great earthquake
- Great Babylon was divided in three parts and fell
- Every island fled away and mountains were not found
- Great hail fell and men blasphemed GOD since the plague was exceedingly great

Revelation [at a glance]
The Eternal State

The Great White Throne Judgment (vv. 19:1 - 20:15)

- Begins after the war of Armageddon
- Those who survive Armageddon (the saints) are judged (Rev. 7:9-17)
- The Books, including the Book of Life are opened and the dead are judged according to their works, by the things written in the Book
- Anyone not found in the Book of Life are cast into the lake of fire
- Those of the 'first resurrection' (144,000) will reign with Christ for a thousand years
- During the thousand years, Satan, his angels, and demons are loosed and goes out to deceive the saints
- Satan will be casted into the lake of fire and his followers will be devoured by fire from heaven
- Those of the 'second resurrection' (the rest of the dead) are judged
- The beast and false prophet are cast in the lake of fire.
- Death and hades are cast into the lake of fire

A New Heaven and A New Earth (vv. 21:1-7)

- There is no more seas
- No more death, neither sorrow, nor crying; no more pain; former things are passed away
- The fountain of the water of life freely given to him who thirsts
- He who overcomes shall inherit all things and be GOD's son

The New Jerusalem (vv. 21:11-27)

- Has no temple
- No need of the sun or moon to shine in it; for the glory of GOD illuminated it
- There will be no night
- Notions of those who are saved shall walk in its light [those who are written in the Lamb's Book of Life]
- Its structure:
    o Great and high walls with twelve gates (three in the east, three in the west, three in the south, three in the north) and twelve angels at each and names of the twelve tribes of the children of Israel written on them
    o Wall has twelve foundations with names of twelve apostles on the Lamb
    o The foundations of the wall of the city were adorned with all kinds of precious stones
    o The construction of its wall was of jasper; and the city was pure gold, like clear glass
    o Twelve gates were as twelve pearls
    o Streets were pure gold, like transparent glass

The River of Life (vv. 22:1-2)

- A pure river of water of life, clear as crystal
- Proceeding from the Throne of GOD and of the Lamb
- The tree of life:
    o In the middle of its street and on either side of the river
    o Bore twelve fruits, each tree yielding its fruits every month
    o Leaves were for healing of the nations

The Rulers of New Jerusalem (vv. 22:3-5)

- Servants of God
- They shall see His face
- His name shall be on their foreheads
- They shall reign forever and ever

Printed in the United States
By Bookmasters